A Picture's Worth

Other Books by Jim Friedman

Poetry

Standing Alone, Leaning Against - (with Dave Smith), Coverstory books, 2022

JIM FRIEDMAN

A PICTURE'S WORTH

Coverstory books

First published in paperback format by
Coverstory books, 2024

ISBN 978-1-7384693-2-1

Copyright © Jim Friedman 2024

The right of Jim Friedman to be identified as the author of this work has been asserted by them in accordance with the Copyright, Designs and Patents Act 1988.

The cover image is designed by Ian Gouge utilising the Adobe suite of products.

All rights reserved.

No part of this publication may be reproduced, circulated, stored in a system from which it can be retrieved, or transmitted in any form without the prior permission of the publisher in writing.

www.coverstorybooks.com

Contents

Words and Music

A book from California	7
'Music for a while...'	8
Lull	9
Poet	10
Imagining Ted Kooser	11

'the isle is full of noises'

Prospero	15
The Mariners	16
Ferdinand and Miranda	17
Caliban	18
Ariel	19

Pictures into Words (1)

Ekphrasis	23
Death of the Virgin	24
Dürer's gloves	25
Samson in furs?	26
'Painted in everlasting colours'	27
Sketch	28

Relics

Ancient	31
Egyptian Mummy	33
"on three legs in the evening"	34
Doctor Dee's mirror	35
Icons	37
Misericords	39

Bestiary

Tyger	43
A hare's form	44
His ways	45
Floaters	46

Aftermaths

Afterwards	49
Ravel's Le Tombeau de Couperin	50
The composer George Butterworth (1885-1916), Morris dancing	51
A Suicide	53
Dally (for JT)	55
Gap	56

Fullness

'the fulness thereof' – a rhapsody	59
Nocturne	60
Footloose	61
Glass with Two White Roses	62
Japanese Garden	63
A moment	64

Pictures into Words (2)

A walk around Nicholas Hilliard (1547-1619)

Hilliards	67
Painting in little.	68
Nicholas Hilliard, self-portrait	69

Joan Eardley (1921-1963), Scottish Painter

Life Drawing	70
Three children at a tenement window	71
Fishing Nets	72
Catterline in Winter	73
Seascapes	74
En plein air	75
Words and paintings	76

✽

Acknowledgements	79

This collection is dedicated to Dave, Emmaline, Ian, Isabel, Joe, Martin, Phil, Roy and Simon – fellow members of the Derby Stanza, for their humour, honesty and encouragement.

Words and Music

A book from California

The door-bell rang and on the mat,
shrink-wrapped in plastic, there it was,
as though delivered by a ghost,
the schedule-conscious courier
just disappearing out the gate.

On a flimsy slip of paper,
its edges browning like the book,
Eileen's decided that it's Good,
the book's materials, that is:
no stains, scrawls, inked-in aperçus.

Diligent doctor, Eileen's checked
the paper jacket's still in-tact,
the spine, the off-white lungs of leaves,
grazes the cloth skin has endured.
All's Good, fit as five dollars gets.

A bill-of-health and billet-doux
from Eileen to a buyer's heart,
enough a come-on to intrigue,
winking its approval like a date
the two of us are setting up.

And there's that musty old book smell
of acid paper, ink and dust,
inhaled each time I open it.
Another Good the poet left,
breath of the ghost he has become.

'Music for a while...'

Two or three, listening to each other
playing, in a room listening to them
playing, the performance in between.

Bird-watching attentiveness to notes
on the air, their murmurations
rising through the dreamed labyrinths they make

and dissolve, falling pagewards like black rain.
Listeners who wonder what they have heard
inside themselves, between, beneath the notes.

Not all cares were beguiled, or even postponed,
their minotaurs restless in the passageways,
dying to hear the twangling played again –

that distant heartsease heard about their ears –
like an escape from sorrows' maze,
following thread, or a fuse burning down.

Lull
(after Debussy's *Prélude á l'aprés midi d'un faune*)

The sun emerges from a street of cloud
as brassy as a band parade
but much too far away to hear.

And comes a lull in the rain,
like a diamond necklace slipping off.
Air retunes and there's a swash and sway

of leaves, a scattering of dapple now
that's semaphoring gold-black-gold,
bright coins flashing on a busker's case.

The fluting of a lonely bird –
cool silver dropping through the canopy
like rain-drips pittering.

The afternoon is glimmer, hologram,
dissolves like asprin to a haze.
And distances beyond this douse

of song are softening, the heat
is opening its oven-door.
Light on my eyelids like a *contre-jour*.

Poet

He lived frugally. Fed himself
from his own garden. Dwelt alone
in a two-roomed wooden house.
Used his life to write poetry.

He kept all his rejection slips.
When he had hundreds of them
he burnt most, no longer caring,
but saved some to write poems on.

There's a glimpse of him peering out
behind others in a photo.
Just a shadowed profile, somehow
all the more evidently there.

Imagining Ted Kooser

Not for him adventurous charts,
or wrestled angels, words
that shape-shift; just a beating heart's
small warmth to guide him as it slips
inside his voice – a startled bird's
outburst of flight moist on his lips.

He says that there are happy afters,
and they're now: family, place,
routines and marriage are rafters
that will keep rain out, your barn warm;
provide a little safety, space
to bide each unexpected storm.

He chronicles mid-western pride.
To him a barn's collapse
is never just a ruin, dreams have died.
Unsettled senses try the locks,
folks for miles around twist their taps
tighter, make sure to wind their clocks.

These local revelations show
he is the pioneer
who stays at home, lets strange stars go,
writes about abandoned, rusting cars.
One of the magi is living here
who follows indigenous stars.

'The Isle Is Full of Noises'

(Shakespeare, *The Tempest*)

Prospero

The poet read his work outdoors;
an audience seated in rows,
heads like skittle-tops below him
in the camera's close-up frame.

Nervous, just audible, he chose
poems about parents and close
friends, loved places lost to the past.
Finishing one, he quickly passed

on to the next. And all the while,
somewhere behind the voice, the smile
crinkling eyes and mouth, a blackbird's
singing could be heard, threading his words

with silver, on and on, as though
Ariel to his Prospero.

The Mariners

The outer movements are wild arabesques,
trills, melismas and turbulence.
The flautist is made to take risks;
his breathing sounds like violence

working its way out of his chest,
as if someone else breathes through him,
some panicky ventriloquist
keening on the brim of a scream.

But the slow movement in between
is water trickling and sunlight
falling through leaves, breeze-ruffled sheen
of grass, soft murmuring at night:

just audible, smoky fluttering
of moths, of candles puttering.

Ferdinand and Miranda

Like a thin, high note held on violins,
a jet-trail drawing new horizons.

Immense emptiness, an up-lit, paling sky
where invisible planes are getting high

on octane, tracing through the air
an evanescent thoroughfare.

It might be litmus paper turning blue,
an alkali dawn, or a coming to –

walking a suburban street, hand-in-hand
with who you are and feeling life is grand,

going places like the wind, birds;
intoxicating, loving words

suddenly working their magic in you,
like contrails opening out of the blue.

Caliban

You give answers to questions we don't hear,
your interviewer out of sight.
Before the camera you appear
uncomfortable and whatever might

have prompted your clear but edgy response
we have to guess at. It's as
if we're witnessing a séance,
where something hidden is rippling the arras.

You unfurl your voice like a yellow rose,
or sunlight lighting up a glass
of water; music no one knows
shining in you like undiscovered stars.

When you open your mouth, out of it come
voices, spirits finding their way back home.

Ariel

Plastic bag, shushing itself as the wind's
eye catches its collapse – now whoosh it goes,
lifts, curtseys, whirls – unfolding as a mind's
attention floats, dips, teeters on tip-toes

over the drive – suddenly snatched on high,
and higher still, up like a hoisted fish
now this way, that, and this across the sky,
descending like a disillusioned wish.

And then it finds a second wind, inhales
and doesn't let it out – white-cheeked balloon,
gone soaring up, past roof, past chimney stack;

a tiny cloud not knowing where it sails,
away, beyond, gone reaching for the moon
above tomorrows. It's not coming back.

Pictures Into Words (1)

Ekphrasis

"really good paintings / make me want to write poetry"
"the lips of the paint are sealed" (David Scott)

'A picture's worth a thousand words'.
Curious to know a few of them,

a buzzing starts up in my mind.
Phrases are dancing on my tongue,

and paintings' sealed lips open slightly.
Curiosity's like kissing them,

tasting their thin silences,
a mouthful of braille bees.

Death of the Virgin
(Pieter Breugel the Elder, 1564)

The room is packed with kneeling folk,
their covered heads like cobblestones
down-trodden by their sadness now.

We see the anguishes of faith
that gathers them to say goodbye
to Mary, dying to the world

and looking once more like a girl.
By her bed, saints like satellites
orbit her flaring-white full moon.

She seems about to self-combust
for soon a miracle begins.
A blinding brightness will eclipse

them all, save Mary, radiant
when angels come – the story goes –
and Jesus takes his mother home.

On the hearth, foreground left,
smoke whirls like a small tornado.
Beside it a figure snores.

Her mouth's a soporific O.
She's given too much of herself
slouching there like a toppled pawn.

Her body's flame a dim tea-light.
She snores at Cape Canaveral,
just as Ascension's lifting off.

Tiredly present and incorrect,
she could be anyone of us –
an "I was there" who missed it all.

Dürer's gloves

'I painted this aged 26'.
You can hear the boast, the pride.
No trumpet's- but a cornet's-worth of toot –
he holds back *just* or *only* twenty six –
stylishly lettered near the hands
on a portrait of himself. The one
with yellow gloves – those look-at-me kid gloves,
their suppleness so softened that
his fingernails show through. His shirt
décolleté, hat and tunic matched,
his hair dishevelled, carefully,
present him as Italian that day
in fourteen ninety eight,
as Somebody Important, in control
of how he wants to spectacle himself.

He couldn't-care-more, showing-off,
pursing his would-be talkative lips.
Eyes turned aside to us – he grants
the briefest audience drifting past
the *sprezzatura* of himself,
his aura of testosterone in oils.
He crafts a dandified, throw-away pose,
the great Herr Selbstie of his age.

"Alive here on this piece of wooden board,
the look of a man with dreams,
who's fathoms deep, will stay with you
and tantalise your eaves-drop mind."

Then I notice that his gloves are grey –
could centuries have faded them? –
not mustard yellow as I thought,
not even buttercup or daffodil.
I have been gilding lilies, Dürer-style.

Samson in furs?
(Durer, Self-portrait, 1500)

Surely a Samson, not a Christ, and blind
to all save how he sees the world,
a cabinet of curios, himself –
most curious object of them all –
looking so far out, beyond
this frame that's barely holding him,
too small theatre for himself.

The *fons et origo* of rivulets,
his hair is fluent, pouring from his head,
his puissance manifest and coiffed,
no Samson for the shears.

Full-frontal stare, compassionless,
blind eyes accost us, x-ray through.
The face a god might have,
impervious to millenia,
watching time fold, unfold...

Yet there's a date, a century's turn,
the painter twenty-eight, and his the face.
Posters of it will be printed,
sold like an inky caviar
to feed a taste for mesmerising looks.

Who is it at the full, so solidly
filling the frame, intimidating us,
as though he's barging through the wall
and heading templewards to set those hands
against the pillars and then push?

This painted likeness of the man,
named Albrecht Durer, by the same,

'Painted in everlasting colours'
(Durer, self-portrait, 1500)

Why write that on the portrait of himself?

What was he promising – his hope
to fend off ageing's greedy dog,
eager to pick a bone with him?

He'd seen too much of flake and craquelure,
mould-spotted murals, varnish darkening,
colours' diminuendo fade.

No weathered Rembrandt likenesses,
nothing remotely lachrymose,
no tares in the harvest of himself.
No 'This old man...'.

He will not give that dog a bone.

Sketch
(pen, ink, watercolour; c.1518-19)

Scant ink lines make him appear as see-through
emptiness or a mysterious blank.

He wants to be seen like God sees souls.
His self-possession's almost absent here.

Loin-cloth naked, he points to where it hurts,
somewhere inside the rib-cage on his left.

Hardly the Dürer he presents elsewhere.
No costumes can disguise him in this sketch.

His password to that Self invalid now,
illness has compromised his own *virtù*.

He has become a vestige of himself –
reduced to an organ that's troubling him –

watching what time is doing, like a mole
digging inside him, loosening his soil.

Relics

Ancient

A thumb-sized, carved bone
or maybe a tusk;
yellowed, with a face
on it from the Stone
Age, from a subfusc,
remotely ur-place.

Features grimed with dirt
look inked in; a nose,
dashed mouth, the bind
of a cap that skirts
the forehead and those
white eyes looking blind.

Streaked with dents and chipped,
pitted on top, there
are signs of a snap
where a cord was slipped
through a hole? A pear-
shaped drop like a tap-

root into the past;
pared down to a chin,
a pointed, slender
tip, smoothed flat to rest
gently against skin
someone thought tender.

But this artefact,
this whitish eavesdrop
on the past withholds
its stories; its cracked
tongue is a full stop,
its white eyes blindfolds.

Grave-silent, thumb-sized
piece of bone, dangled
from someone's neck or
wrist, maybe once prized
for feelings tangled
in its metaphor.

Egyptian Mummy
(the first object in Neil MacGregor's radio series A History of the World in 100 Objects)

Hornedjitef captains his coffin. Under the lid
are a map of stars and a figured frieze – ship's log
of sailing through the underworld, using a grid
to navigate cold galaxies that fog
his voyage to forever. In his cedar casque,
his amulets about him, organs parcelled up inside,
like post sent to the future, his eternal task
is surfing heavens set before him, starry-eyed.
The figured frieze unrolls like frames of film, showing
him sailing to his own Byzantium, among
protecting gods and useful slaves. This movie, going
round inside the lid, plays to a packed house of one.
Reclining, mummified with unguents and tars,
Hornedjitef is at the pictures, watching stars.

Hornedjitef has stopped in Bloomsbury instead
of heaven. Among the lost and found a hundred years,
he's been dumped as luggage left there by the dead,
enduring endless sample-takers, probes and smears.
Excursions to a hospital, to get some rays,
have taken him out of himself. Now, brought to earth,
beneath his cartonnage of black and gold, he displays
his browned bandages, looking like a tuber. Rebirth
becomes a gruesomely forensic comedy,
not ending happily beyond the furthest stars
but here, exhibited half-dressed. The public see
his name-cartouche, his mummy, no canopic jars
but charts of smashed-window stars. Something that hope
might see – or children draw – lacking a telescope.

"on three legs in the evening"

The hundred or so carved
walking-sticks in his tomb,
like a picket-fence.

Beyond the lapis, gold
and onyx-stone, his throne
and inlaid chariots,

someone remembered this –
how he leaned to one side
eavesdropping on the air –

was sceptical enough
to think the afterlife
might not be different:

treading the earth at noon,
not as the Sphinx riddled
but walking on three legs,

tapping earth like a jug
he fills with thuds of full,
echoes of emptiness.

Doctor Dee's mirror

Inch-thick: the mirror of Philosophy.
Bigger than a paten-dish,
it can be hung upon a wall indoors,
appears a moon enduring an eclipse.
Most wondrous is how smooth it is;
like silk stretched over stone,
a pool of smoky ink, icy to touch.

Rarer than that *mummia*, dust of kings,
its substance is obsidian,
that Pliny wrote of in his History.
Black, glassy oozings, some say angel's blood –
adept for scrying apparitions,
glimmers in this lake of darkness,
in this pupil of the Lord.

From the depths elusively, like fish,
they rise; pursed on their lips,
they raise a kiss towards the brim,
a bubble of empyrean,
hosannah-speech that angels use.

The fundament of bats has polished this.
For weeks the tiny fricatives
of insect wings, minutest skeletons
brushed up against its eye, have rubbed
the world away like milky cataracts,
infusing this dark stone with aerial
intelligence, waiting to be spoken,
ghostly answers flapping at this glass –
the door to magisterium.

Witnesses have sworn, on oath,
they have conversed with seraphim,
so puissant is the mystery
divines most practised in the art
of Seeing reach, possessing this.

Think of your own good self
reflected in its sheen, that spirits may
cognise the fisherman who angles there,
obedient to your will alone.
The great arcanum waits for you.

John Dee, (1527-1608), was a mathematician, astronomer and occult philosopher.

Icons

Long abstracts of the human face,
blackened and old.
Ovals and curves express a grace,
remote and cold,

as if a candle lights the dark
in high relief,
incising faces with a stark,
sinuous grief.

Gold discs and crescents, burnished spoons
of holiness;
the halos round their heads are moons
that almost kiss.

Madonna holds her seated Christ
upon her arm;
out on the limb of her tense wrist,
he is her psalm.

Her face tilts down to greet his lips
but she stares past
us, looking to the dark eclipse
and the lots cast.

An arc, from eyebrow down the nose,
shifts to one side
the focus of her still repose.
Her features slide

towards the child whom she can feed
but only look
upon his otherwordly need
like a dark book.

Icons are flowers from a far
country's rich dirt
somewhere inside of us. They are
rooted in hurt,

the bitter soils of it crumbling
on lips – a share
of black bread for silent mumbling
like a prayer.

Misericords

In this nether world,
chiselled, time-burnished reliefs
bulge out of the wood

below the choir stalls –
oak lustred to caramel,
toffee-apple gloss.

Peeking underneath
the seats was meant to feel
like lifting a lid

on neighbours' follies,
their bum-bare antics
flies on walls would blush at.

Glimpses through key-holes,
poor folk trying to get by,
things seen bottom-up –

wives scolding husbands,
song-birds mobbing owls, and carts
in front of horses.

Upside down misrule,
vignettes of charivari
jostle with the saints.

Wood-carver's satire
in amongst the reverence –
laughter in the dark,

audible as farts.
Jokers in the pack snigger
under bums on seats.

Knobbly surfaces
crust the wood like pastry shapes
baked on a great pie.

Bestiary

Tyger

Sumatran tiger, huge
assemblage of muscle,
thick panniers of it,
haltingly you lurch
on the stump of your leg,
your fearful symmetry
disarranged by poachers
hunting for body-parts.

Rangers display the skins
kept in formaldehyde,
like wet jumpsuits, onesies
stored for this grotesque show
of floppy limbs – legs, paws,
wired right through like cheeses.
Magnificence crumpled
to these deflated scraps.

Your coat like a bar-code
in greed's supermarket,
what would you say to Blake,
or Lawrence, lord of life,
looking out from the cage
where you lie awkwardly,
tail steadily lashing
striped shadows on the floor?

A hare's form

The sitting tenant having fled,
the discovery afterwards,

like reading a private letter
left behind, lying on the floor

where life had written on its page.
Earth-dent, concavity, a scrape

of settlement, slight on the ground,
in grass, the shape of rest and nest,

a flatness documenting pause,
an act of sitting out from flux –

like a spoon in tussocky green tea.
Hardly a saucerful, a sip

already cooling. A hare's breadth
between life and nothingness. Read the lips,

the worked earth is an open mouth
the creature's slipped from like a word,

a syllable to conjure with,
softly breathed, almost a sigh,

elusive as the life it calls,
hastily camouflaged elsewhare.

His ways

His cold nose in my eye,
loud purring in my face,
peremptory pawing
at duvet, pillow, cheek.
If all these fail, he tries
to smother me with fur.

This first-light repertoire
of ways to get me up
and heading for his bowl
eventually succeeds
and he Pied Pipers me
downstairs to get his food.

And waiting to go out,
it's absolutely clear
the cat-flap's infra dig.
For comings and goings,
a doorman is required.
And guess who gets the job?

On his return he wants
a cushion – me. Side-flopped
heavily on my chest,
he leans against my arm
and cradled there he rests
an ear against my heart.

A little déjà vu
perhaps, reminiscent
of that beat he knew once
weeks inside his mother.
A lost togetherness
he needs an echo of.

Floaters

Perpendicular whales,
like giant aubergines
asleep in the sea's loft.

Groups of them, hanging there,
buoyantly suspended
like static mobiles.

As upright as dolmens,
they slumber silently,
enormously tired out,

becalmed in the doldrums
of their dreams – dark floaters
on the eye of the sea.

Aftermaths

Afterwards

He cries for others, for himself,
dry and silent. A photograph
of him would look like he's laughing.

As though at the pictures, he sits
in the dark where they come for him
in the ghost of his uniform.

Or he conjures them nearer,
like nervous creatures, men he knew,
much closer to them in the dark.

He didn't know them very long,
remembers though when they approach
his cenotaph one by one.

There at his shoulder as he writes,
he nurses the faith he had in them,
the one sure love he's ever felt.

A caustic haunting while it hurts
to think of all they might have been,
the afterwards of his long life.

Ravel's *Le Tombeau de Couperin*

Tombeau for those he knew,
his grief disguised as charm.
He lifts them up, they dance,
each leaning on his arm
like the pliant marionettes
of men in the ambulance
he drove who leant upon him, too.

This is the hospital
they never reached, where sounds
familiar to them
let us dream a little
while of dancing. No ambulance,
no pain, no telegram,
tersely phrased, saying 'died of wounds'.

Elegance and grace
make music to outstay
old Death who's envious
of dance – when people face
each other, whirling round and round,
all but oblivious
of something he's trying to say.

The composer George Butterworth (1885-1916), Morris dancing

Dressed in white, as if a ghost danced,
with bell-pads on his legs; hankies,
maybe napkins, flourished like flags
waving some joyous surrender.

He jumps, skips, puts his right foot forward,
toeing the imaginary
waters of the *High Town Jig*,
its tune a line of stepping stones

he lights on like an organist,
treading the pedals of the dance.
The film stops with him in mid-air,
jumping into a blur of white flash.

And then comes *Hey Boys Up We Go*.
Four of them wind and wind about
through figures of eight. George collides
with Cecil and they both guffaw.

Droopy-thick moustaches can't obscure
his laughter as he creases up,
smiles to the unknown cameraman,
inviting him to share the fun.

It's summer – flowers in a light-
strafed border – shut inside a box
in 1912. His liveliness
kept on thousands of picture cards

flicked through the Kinora machine
as if shuffling a haunted deck.
He is the Joker in the pack,
kitted with bells; no peaked cap yet.

He keeps on dancing in my head,
in khaki now, sure-footed tread
on duckboards, stepping over men.
There's a blurred flash. He creases up.

The Kinora machine was an early form of motion picture device, invented by the brothers Lumière in 1896. The Kinora reels were manufactured in Britain from 1902 (Wikipedia).

A Suicide

Why?
a question in a cul de sac,
just nowhere to go with it,
more likely too many places:
anger, guilt, regrets backed up,
jamming a road suddenly closed off.

Questions –
like warning signs, flapping tape,
screens – cordon off an area
as if trying to cover up
an empty space, your absence
too naked to be left exposed.

If onlys...
how come we didn't read your mind,
touch your failing heart, listen
to silences getting heavier,
unbudgeable as stones, needing
to be lifted, held in someone's arms?

Forgive us,
coming late like this, after closing time,
with cups of thirst you cannot quench
when all you had was vinegar.
Now we have tea and sandwiches
and find it difficult to think of you.

Not ready
to live with what we didn't know,
our love for you hurts, is tight-lipped,
and murmurs here like something slowly
going underground. We're afraid
of what will grow up in its place.

And angry
you've taken us with you into darkness
we can get out of, unlike you
swallowed by a black hole, never coming back.
We live with an everlasting bruise.
Touching it draws us nearer to you.

Dally (for JT)

In the blue hallway
shadows mimed long days
outside the window,
summer's gaudiness
endlessly burning.

From the large garden,
occasions murmured,
faintly brushing walls.

Weeks snailed past his cries.

Behind a closed door,
he lapped from toilets,
waiting for rescue;
paring down nine lives
to a pea-small turd.

Calls, leaflets, whistling;
candles lit for him
kept what was to come
unsure, still open.

Brief years later, thin,
gauntly muscular,
climbing for dear life –
ladders, pergolas –
he used himself up:
defiant spendthrift,
soft purse full of change.

Gap

Square, squat chimneys
like enormous teeth
gape in silhouette
where the road turns out
to the rouged sky.

The way between
white-washed cottages
finds a narrow gap
you have to drive through
taking your own time,

barely noticing
dusk-light deepening
as the sunset dips
a cataracted yolk
just over rooftops.

A moment piercing
a needle's eye, then
out beyond yourself,
feeling old settlements
shifting one last time.

The road unhedges
like shoulders loosening,
hill-slopes wing up
sheer each side of you,
as though lifting off.

You drive into darkness,
disappearing down
a slip of valley road –
that final magic trick
we have in each of us.

Fullness

'the fulness thereof' – a rhapsody

moonlit belly of a gravid hare
white egg of fur a purse
for leverets the futures they will live
rarely seen something to have faith in

and that's the bulb-life of a womb
a foetus in its amniotic hold
now brimming in the cup of genesis
about to pour a new life out

O yonge fresshe folkes he and she*
their candle flames are blown about
how bright they are how earnestly they sound
look hope is on them like the dew

late August sun a breath of wind
the borders colouring themselves
with crayonny exuberance
hot sundae for a gardener's trug

comet on its grand circumference
a horizontal avalanche
effervescing thorough space
come round to where it started from

the wondrous moment makes you rise
extend your arms up widely to the sky
as though a planet's lowering itself
like fruit into your arms

* *Chaucer, "Troilus and Criseyde"*

Nocturne
(after Skating by moonlight, c.1950, Ronald Lampitt (1906-88)

No ordinary wonder of a moon –
a search-light left on in this nursery
where we are lifted up inside a dream,

as birds are, perched in a bright evening,
over the playground of a frozen pond,
sashed with a strip of shining ice.

Tinter of silver, bluish-grey and white,
like breathing on a frosty night,
brings alive the coldness there.

The only grown-ups are tall trees –
grandparents who have seen it all before.
They overlook the goings-on,

where adults feel translated back,
skating through childhoods once again
while their kids fall and laugh out loud.

A small dog barks to see such fun
as boys skate away to the shine
unrolling there across the pond.

All are playing a joyful game,
their toy-like figures on a tablecloth
of lit-up snow that's paused in time.

The night bestows this gift on those
who gather once on this blue-moon,
skating as though they walk on air.

Footloose
(for Heinz)

No mobile phones back then, no maps, just paths
to follow, taking the first boat that came
to other islands I knew nothing of,
sleeping rough on beaches, anywhere
secluded I could get away with it.

Penniless, unwashed for weeks, without food
for days, mind-numbingly exhausted
after eighteen hours walking to a port,
I've never felt so radiantly free
since that first solo holiday abroad.

The memory of it is a souvenir
picked up, held for a second, for the dream
it has become: smoothed, burnished by years
of touching it, turning its hologram
of me this way and that, seeing it change.

It seems I lived a kind of poetry:
walking each day like writing a new line,
not quite sure what would come along, at each turn
on the road, excitedly discovering
a fresh aliveness giving me its word.

Glass with Two White Roses
(photograph, Taizo Kato c.1920)

A rose stem leaning from a glass.
A few leaves
then it arches out up to its rose.

Soft-focus petals kiss the light,
composing
paper-like crescents, lips of pearl.

A rosebud on the table, stem
refracted
through half empty water in the glass.

Let's say a photograph of time,
stopping here
over a century ago.

And also loss – now budded rose,
now open
cup of petals reaching over it –

small difference that's showing us
the short while
perfection has, no time at all.

The table top's dark sheen reflects
blurred roses
seeming to glow through fog,

like someone's vague remembering
of flowers,
briefly beautiful in a glass.

Japanese Garden

Visitors pause,
like figures brushed
delicately
on a silk screen.

Angular rocks
arranged just so,
like small islands
in a combed sea

of gravel stones
gardeners card
through carefully
with bamboo rakes.

The views arrange
and change themselves
as I step round
cleanly swept paths.

The silence here
holds onto pond-
water trickling
to further ponds.

Dew – as the air
distils its breath
on surfaces –
beads along leaves.

Thoughts like water-
boatmen floating
on a taut skin
of quietness.

A moment

Just moonlit roof-tiles on a barn,
their slate-sheen fuzzed with frost –
a silvered etching in mid air.

The night's stillness made visible,
blank and beyond peaceful,
the cold gift of it like a grace,

unwarranted. A blessing of the light
putting words in the night's mouth –
silence, crystal, silver, frost.

Pictures Into Words (2)

A walk around Nicholas Hilliard (1547-1619)

Hilliards

From ovals small as eyes,
pearl-earringed men look out,
elaborately dressed
in ruffs and rakish hats.

Lilliputian men
to fit a lover's hand,
much as a jewel would
reposing on a palm.

They hold an audience,
invite us to admire
their doublets slashed with gills
exhaling puffs of silk.

Or they're déshabillé,
in linen white as pain,
yearning against a wall
of ostentatious flames.

Brushwork with a single hair
captures spun-sugar lace
rust and moth will not eat,
features that will not age:

little arcadias
of their only springtime
where they are always green,
in love with what they are.

Painting in little.

I woo the gentlemen,
arouse their swaggering

and serve them good opinions
of themselves and me.

For faces, just one hair
tickles them to the life –

witness my self-portrait's
mustachios and curls .

To avoid disturbing
dust, I barely breathe,

have windows nailed, wear silks,
stand absolutely still.

Sitters take a deep breath,
hold it in for centuries.

Amongst their finery
a tiny face peeps out

from ruffs, brocade, slashed silks,
the wrappings of their lives.

I think of mummy-cloths,
shrouds, cocooning them

like parcels to be sent
into the future.

On playing cards I paint
queens, jacks. Sometimes knaves.

Nicholas Hilliard, self-portrait
I have not seen a dapper jack so brisk (Marlowe, Edward II)

He wears a pleated ruff,
wide as a dinner plate.
His head's served up on it –
tangles of snowflakes
swarming round his neck.

Someone has clumsily
retouched the intricate
lace filigree. It shows,
ironically, how
much better Hilliard was

with a single-haired brush
and very steady hand,
scarcely breathing at all
for fear of raising dust
while painting flakes of lace.

He stares at us aslant,
as if we posed for him
already. Sketching us,
his eyes would be jet beads
abacussing to and fro

and we the dartboard
where his glances quiz.
Marlovianly *brisk*,
his portrait doth present
the dapperest of jacks –

teased curls and combed moustache
delicately brushed on.
Acorns and oak leaves fringe
his cap, as if to say
'From little things, great oaks'.

Joan Eardley (1921-1963), Scottish Painter

Life Drawing

She stands there, waiting to begin,
trousered legs firmly planted.
Looking across her drawing board,
she waits for the tide coming in,

brimming eye, then hand, then paper,
with its own fresh necessity.
Holding her charcoal like a burnt
offering, she lets the tide shape her,

feeling it getting cold, colder
as it surfaces out of her,
bulging through the drawing-paper,
into thighs, midriff, a shoulder.

Three children at a tenement window
(gouache) 1956

She loved to paint children,
later the sea. Both deep,
constantly in motion,
volatile creatures,
voraciously alive.

She draws kids as cartoons
just stepped down from a wall,
charcoaled and coloured in.
Reds, greens float over them
like sunshine, in and out.

White net-curtain, catching
a breeze, lifts slightly;
it resembles etched glass,
damask as letters scrawled
on the tenement's stones.

A kind of signature,
they leave here, while they can.
The city rubs them out
like chalk, wipes off their smiles.
She has them stare at her,

at us, uncertainly,
as they might the future.
They prefer their comics,
so she paints them reading,
faces turned, miles away.

Fishing Nets

At Catterline they peak and scoop, the nets
like longships prowing up the sands, almost
the choppy sea itself, spread out, floating,
a see-through simulacrum of the waves

washing at your doorstep, rinsing the beach
beneath your cottage of its pitiful
spillages, dragging back its loneliness.
Nets like a cast taken from the sea's face -

anguish moving back and forth, not knowing
what to do with itself, where to be at rest.
You struggled with the sea to hold it still;
the empty nets full of its upheaval.

Catterline in Winter
(oil on hardboard) 1963

At first sight, a toy train's making its way
down the cold slope
under a sky of dingy, blackboard grey,
and there's no hope

of winter letting go anytime soon,
no chance of thaw.
That comet-like smudge of white could be a moon,
perhaps a raw

turnip-slice of sun. Scumbled pack-ice shows
a twist of road.
The toy train's carriages metamorphose
to a spilt load

of cottages; black, boxy rectangles
toppling downhill.
All's slant and slither beyond scribbled tangles
of grass, sea-squill.

Locked, shut down moment of exhausted calm
after the storm.
Drawn-in breath – tomorrow's safe from harm,
tight in its corm.

Seascapes

Then, at the last, the sea outside her door,
stirring its creams and tars,
the slop and slap of waves churning
sea-butter while she spars
with paints and the gale winds' full-on roar.

Obsessively in love with the driving
winter sea, with its rough-
shod, apocalyptic weather,
she's overboard enough
to paint like a castaway. She's re-living

each drowning wave where it falls and scatters;
a survivor out of breath,
just managing to reach the shore,
who knows this brush with death
on canvas is all that really matters.

En plein air

An easel in front of the sea;
you paint the tumult happening:
wave-surge, light swatching through its book
of weather, and the waves' white toil.

It's like a playground. Seismic shifts
of feral children rise and fall
on the climbing frame of the sea,
screaming as you wrap them in oils

when they have hurt themselves on rocks,
or had a tantrum on the beach –
ruins of bladder-wrack and driftwood,
smashed up messes from the sea's floor.

A photograph of you painting,
silhouetted against a white
slather of waves. On your canvas
the view repeated, minus you.

Words and paintings
(after Howard Hodgkin, 1932-2017)

1.

There's this thing of oils and wood,
glue, canvas, nails, eyelets and wire
with a vision painted on one side,

like the face of a moon. You feel
its tides in you, its gravity
distending you like nothing else can;

save for the painter's words scribbled
on the back like a billet-doux
for the purchaser's eyes only.

And there's a curator's note –
identifying artist, title, date –
displayed on a gallery wall:

lines tethering these moons docked here
for admiration and for sale.
They unload the journeys they dared

as colours – meditated on
for months while left facing a wall,
like children trying to be good.

2.

The titles are umbilical,
trailing to moments
they were born,
whereas the paintings block

their subjects into coloured shapes –
ice-cream pink, yellow for a dress,
grey – listening to music rain.

The words and paints rub side by side,
like differently purposed boats
sandpapering each other's hulls.

The gull-cries over them are us –
excited, clamorously calling out
as colours bob and float their wares.

There's no Rosetta stone for this
but we try out our Linear B
for turning pictures into words.

Acknowledgements

- "Painting in Little" was initially published in *New Contexts: 4*, Coverstory books (2022)
- "Icons" was initially published in *New Contexts: 5*, Coverstory books (2023)

Special thanks to Ian Gouge who's example has been an inspiration and who generously agreed to publish this collection.

A warm thank you to members of the Derby Stanza group. Many of these poems have benefitted from their perceptive feedback.

Milton Keynes UK
Ingram Content Group UK Ltd.
UKHW020841030624
443491UK00013B/253